LAMAR AND MAYA
Build A Robot

Copyright © 2023 by Siohan Press

Written By Auntie Sierra

All rights reserved. No part of this book may be used or reproduced in any manner whatsoever without prior written permission of the author.
contact@siohanpress.com

ISBN 978-1-959451-95-2

Siohan Press
www.siohanpress.com

Today is the day that Lamar and Maya build a robot.

They are friends and love to build together.

They go to the living room to get started.

Maya opens the box. "There are so many parts," she says.

Lamar sees the large square with the buttons. "What does this part do?" he asks.

"That is the controller," says Maya. "It is like your brain for the robot."

They also find some parts that have a cable.

"Those are the motors," says Maya.

What is this part that looks like a camera?" says Lamar.

That is the color sensor. It detects colors.

It is now time to assemble all the parts to build the robot.

Maya chooses a robot design.

Lamar has the instructions and is ready to build.

He finds the parts for step one and puts them together.

Lamar goes to the next step. He finds the parts and adds them to the robot.

Maya helps with the instructions to make sure they are following the steps.

Oh no! Lamar cannot find the red part with the five holes on step nine.

"Where is this red part?" he says to Maya.

They look on the floor.

They look in the box.

They look in the box again.

This time they find the missing part.

Now they have all the parts for step nine.

They add them to the robot.

Maya goes to the next step.

Lamar helps her find the parts.

After many steps, Maya is almost done.

She adds the last part to the robot.

"This is cool!" says Lamar.
"We built a robot!"

"What will we make the robot do?" he says to Maya.

Made in the USA
Middletown, DE
21 March 2024